8/06

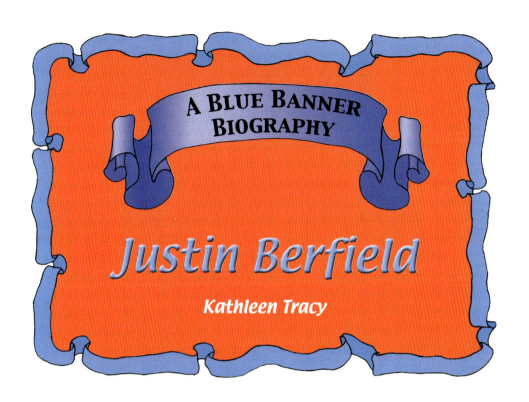

A BLUE BANNER
BIOGRAPHY

Justin Berfield

Kathleen Tracy

Mitchell Lane
PUBLISHERS

P.O. Box 196
Hockessin, Delaware 19707
Visit us on the web: www.mitchelllane.com
Comments? email us: mitchelllane@mitchelllane.com

Printing   1   2   3   4   5   6   7   8   9

Blue Banner Biographies

Alicia Keys	Allen Iverson	Ashanti
Ashton Kutcher	Ashlee Simpson	Avril Lavigne
Beyoncé	Bow Wow	Britney Spears
Carrie Underwood	Christina Aguilera	Christopher Paul Curtis
Clay Aiken	Condoleezza Rice	Daniel Radcliffe
Derek Jeter	Eminem	Eve
Ja Rule	Jay-Z	Jennifer Lopez
J. K. Rowling	Jodie Foster	**Justin Berfield**
Kate Hudson	Lance Armstrong	Lindsay Lohan
Mario	Mary-Kate and Ashley Olsen	Melissa Gilbert
Michael Jackson	Missy Elliott	Nelly
Paris Hilton	P. Diddy	Queen Latifah
Ritchie Valens	Rita Williams-Garcia	Ron Howard
Rudy Giuliani	Sally Field	Selena
Shirley Temple	Usher	

Library of Congress Cataloging-in-Publication Data
Tracy, Kathleen.
        Justin Berfield / by Kathleen Tracy.
                p. cm. – (A blue banner biography)
        Includes bibliographical references and index.
        ISBN 1-58415-392-X (lib. bd.)
        1. Berfield, Justin—Juvenile literature. 2. Actors—United States—Biography—
Juvenile literature. I. Title. II. Series.
PN2287.B4329T73 2005
792. 02'8'092--dc22

                                                                                2005009688

ABOUT THE AUTHOR: Kathleen Tracy has been a journalist for over twenty years. Her writing has been featured in magazines including *The Toronto Star's* "Star Week," *A&E Biography* magazine, *KidScreen*, and *TVTimes*. She is also the author of numerous biographies including "The Boy Who Would be King" (Dutton), "Jerry Seinfeld - The Entire Domain" (Carol Publishing), "Don Imus - America's Cowboy" (Carroll & Graf), "Mariano Guadalupe Vallejo," and "William Hewlett: Pioneer of the Computer Age," both for Mitchell Lane. She has recently completed "Diana Rigg: The Biography" for Benbella Books.

PHOTO CREDITS: Cover, p. 4— courtesy of Justin Berfield; pp. 10, 12, 16 — courtesy of Justin Berfield; p. 21 WireImage; p. 22 — courtesy of Justin Berfield; p. 28 Getty Images
PUBLISHER'S NOTE: This story has been authorized and approved for publication by Justin Berfield and his manager Jason Felts. Part of the proceeds from the sale of this book have been donated to the Ronald McDonald House Charities at Justin's request.

CONTENTS

Growing up on a hit television series means Justin is always being recognized by fans. "Sometimes girls will come up to me and ask if I am that kid from the show. But it's fun. I like meeting other people."

Helping Others

*A*s Reese, the second oldest sibling on *Malcolm in the Middle,* Justin Berfield plays a character known more for fighting than helping others. It just shows how good of an actor Justin is because in real life, he is a devoted volunteer for the Ronald McDonald House Charities.

Justin first got involved with the charity by participating in a fundraiser for the Loma Linda Ronald McDonald House in southern California. Every year the LLRMH puts on a Mini Grand Prix race to raise money. Then in 2002, he was named the national youth ambassador for RMHC. His primary job was to increase public awareness of the important service the Houses provide families. As ambassador, he visited Ronald McDonald Houses all across the country where he met many kids and their families. He also participated in fundraising events.

"I have always believed in the importance of giving something back, so I am honored to serve as a youth ambassador for Ronald McDonald House Charities," Justin said at the time. "Through my involvement, I hope to let people everywhere learn more about the great work being done by RMHC and encourage young people to participate in charitable efforts."

One of the highlights of that year was being on hand for the announcement of McDonald's first World Children's Day. On that day the company would hold fundraisers in all its 29,000 restaurants in 121 different countries. The money would help children in each restaurant's own community.

"Through my work as a Ronald McDonald House Charities youth ambassador, I have had many incredible and memorable experiences," Justin told reporters at the press conference. "It's very rewarding to know that a program like World Children's Day has been created to help children around the world in need, and right in our own neighborhoods at places like this Ronald McDonald House."

The charity got its start in 1973 when two parents named Fran and Fred Hill got some very bad news.

> *"I have always believed in the importance of giving something back,"* Justin said.

Their three-year-old daughter Kim was diagnosed with leukemia, a cancer of the bone marrow. Bone marrow is a substance inside bones that produces the blood cells eveyone needs to live and be healthy.

Kim underwent treatment for leukemia. She had to stay at the hospital for weeks at a time while the doctors tried to make her better. Her parents were there with her every day. Not wanting to leave their daughter's side, they ate candy bars and whatever other junk food they could find in vending machines. They often slept in chairs in the hospital.

Fred was a football player for the Philadelphia Eagles. He wanted to do something to help.

While at the hospital, they met other parents whose children were sick and getting treatment. Some families had traveled from very far away. Many could not afford to pay for hotel rooms because they spent all their money to pay the doctors and the hospital. Fred was a professional football player for the Philadelphia Eagles. He and Fran wanted to do something to help other parents who weren't as financially fortunate as they were. Their idea was a "home away from home" where families of the sick children could stay and support each other emotionally.

Fred got his teammates and the Eagles organization to donate money. The team also asked the local

McDonald's restaurants to help raise money for their project. McDonald's agreed. Named after the corporation's famous clown, the Ronald McDonald House opened in Philadelphia in 1974.

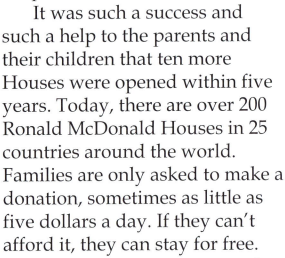

In Justin's case, his fame has made him more humble and more appreciative of what he has.

It was such a success and such a help to the parents and their children that ten more Houses were opened within five years. Today, there are over 200 Ronald McDonald Houses in 25 countries around the world. Families are only asked to make a donation, sometimes as little as five dollars a day. If they can't afford it, they can stay for free.

Sometimes success can make people think they are more special than others. In Justin's case, his fame has made him more humble and more appreciative of what he has.

"I think my parents did a really good job of keeping me grounded," he told the author. "They never let me feel better than anyone else because in reality you are no better than anyone else just because you're on television."

But there is one skill that makes Justin stand out— he was born with a natural ability to act. It didn't take long for the rest of the world to find out.

The Commercial Kid

When many people think of Southern California, they picture a crowded place full of people, cars and smog. But in Oak Park, a picturesque, park-filled community just forty minutes west of Los Angeles, people live in wide-open spaces away from the bustle of the city. Justin Tyler Berfield was born on February 25, 1986 and grew up in Oak Park, which is located beside the Santa Monica Mountains National Recreation Area. The area is home to a variety of wildlife, including coyotes, deer, golden eagles, snakes and even mountain lions.

For an animal lover like Justin, growing up in Oak Park was great because there was plenty of room for his family's menagerie of pets. Over the years, the Berfields have had cats, dogs, chickens, a horse, desert tortoises, goats, a ferret and a pot-bellied pig named Arnold.

Justin is a self-proclaimed animal lover. Here he poses with an iguana that is definitely feeling the Christmas spirit.

Justin even helped his pet pug deliver puppies—twice. At one point he considered becoming a veterinarian. But that was before he realized his true calling.

Some actors say they grew up knowing they wanted to be performers. In Justin's case, some friends of his parents urged him to give acting a try. He quickly discovered it was what he wanted to do.

"Their kids were a year or two older than I was and would go out on auditions," he recalled. "When I was five, I started going with them to auditions and I thought that it looked pretty cool. One time it was an open casting call for a Folgers Coffee commercial where they would be seeing 150 kids. So I went in just pretending I was an actor. For commercial auditions you don't have to do as much as you do for a TV show, so I read the lines and I got it. I was just lucky right off the bat."

> **Within that first year, Justin appeared in almost 20 national television commercials, including ads for McDonalds.**

Within that first year, Justin appeared in more than 20 national television commercials, including ads for McDonalds and Colgate toothpaste. He was so good and was hired so often that casting agents started calling him "The Commercial Kid." His older brother Lorne also started acting around the same time but eventually lost interest.

"He did a few commercials and a movie but he didn't enjoy it as much as I did," Justin explained. "It takes a lot of hard work to sit on a set for eight hours a day and memorize your lines and he just wasn't up for it. But I really enjoyed it so I continued with commercials and TV shows."

In all, Justin would end up doing more than 30 national commercials before landing his first television show. He certainly lived up to his nickname.

Justin comes from a close-knit family. He credits his parents for keeping him from getting a big head. He still has dinner at least once a week with his family. From left to right: his dad Rick, brother Lorne, Justin and his mom Gail.

Justin is quick to point out he couldn't have done it without the help of his family. His dad, Rick, who is a tile contractor, and his mom Gail fully supported and encouraged him.

"It takes a lot," he said. "Without my mom, I wouldn't have been able to go on any interviews. I remember every day after school I'd have to jump in the car and fly to an audition somewhere in downtown L.A. And I would sometimes do three or four auditions a day."

Although getting jobs was fun, learning to deal with not being hired was difficult.

> "The biggest thing to overcome as an actor is getting used to rejection," Justin admitted.

"The biggest thing to overcome as an actor is getting used to rejection," Justin admitted. "You might audition for one hundred roles and not get any of them. And that's the toughest thing to overcome because you'll get called back three times and then at the very end they'll say, 'No, you're not the right look,' so you have to love what you do."

Because he spent all his free time going to auditions or filming, Justin had to give up other activities. One was his martial arts class, where he was a third-degree red belt in Tang Soo Do karate and was good enough to compete in state and national tournaments.

When he was six, those skills helped Justin to be cast in a comedy-action film called *3 Ninjas*. The movie was about three young boys who possess special martial arts skills and take on a gang of criminals. But what had started out as one of his happiest professional moments ended up being a frustrating experience. "My role got cut out so I was really disappointed," he said in a teenhollywood.com online chat in 2001.

> **But what had started out as one of his happiest professional moments ended up being a frustrating experience.**

Even so, Justin refused to get discouraged. "You have to love it no matter what because you never know when you're going to get the role of your life," he said.

And in just a few short years, Justin would find himself getting not just one but two roles of a lifetime.

Justin Goes Primetime

*O*ther than spending so much of his free time driving to and from auditions and filming commercials, Justin's life at home was like any other kid's. He hung out with friends, took care of his pets, watched football and basketball on TV and went fishing with his dad in Malibu whenever possible. "Every weekend we would kayak fish down at the pier," he recalled.

While he was close to both parents, his relationship with his brother was more volatile. He told *Sixteen Magazine* that he and his brother Lorne shared a typical sibling bond: "We'd get along, but we'd also fight. It's weird; we can be the best of friends or the worst of enemies."

Justin made his television series debut in the NBC comedy, *The Good Life*, which premiered in January 1994. The sitcom starred stand-up comic John Caponera and Justin played one of his three sons. Although the show got many good reviews, it went off the air after just thirteen episodes. Justin considered it a great learning experience.

The very next year, when he was nine, Justin was selected to co-star in another mid-season replacement show, the WB sitcom *Unhappily Ever After*. This series would stay on the air for five years and film 100 episodes. Justin played Ross, the youngest but best-adjusted member of the Malloy family. Ross's parents

Fishing is one of Justin's favorite pastimes. He often goes to Cabo San Lucas where his dad owns a vacation home. He loves the beaches and the fact it's so close to Los Angeles so he can fly down for a weekend of fishing and relaxation.

are divorced and his father Jack lives in a dumpy apartment and gets advice from a stuffed rabbit he imagines can talk. The show was set in Van Nuys, California, not far from Justin's real-life hometown.

When Justin wasn't working, he attended Brookside and Sumac Elementary Schools in Oak Park. Because he had to be on the set every day, Justin attended school at the studio and was taught by tutors during the months the show filmed. By law he had to have an average of at least three hours of instruction and couldn't work more than nine and a half hours a day. He was also required to have an adult guardian with him. That meant his mom Gail had to be on the set with him all the time.

While Justin had always found commercial work fun, being on a series brought more responsibility. "The most important traits you need to act are concentration so you can study your lines and be prepared every day and all day long," he said.

Fortunately Justin finds memorizing scripts easy. "I have what I guess you could call a photographic memory," he revealed in his teenhollywood.com chat.

> *While Justin had always found commercial work fun, being on a series brought more responsibility.*

During his time on *Unhappily Ever After* Justin did several movies: *The Kid with X-Ray Eyes*, where he finds a pair of glasses that allows him to see through things; *Mom, Can I Keep Her?* in which a 500-pound gorilla follows him home from school; and the straight-to-video *The Invisible Mom II*, playing a young orphan whose new adoptive mother can turn invisible. In a change of pace, he appeared in the dramatic thriller *Wanted*, which was about a boy who is hiding from criminals in an all-boys' school after witnessing a murder.

In a way, Justin had the best of both worlds. Although he was working regularly, he was still anonymous enough that his success didn't intrude on his personal life. While many people might think he looked familiar when they passed him on the street, hardly anyone knew who he was. That was about to change.

> Not long after "Unhappily Ever After" ended, Justin auditioned for another sitcom to be aired on FOX.

Not long after *Unhappily Ever After* ended, Justin auditioned for another sitcom to be aired on FOX. The creator of the series was Linwood Boomer, a former actor turned writer and producer best known for his work on *Little House on the Prairie*. Called *Malcolm in the Middle*, the show was about an 11-year-old genius and his odd family. "I liked how quirky the characters were," Justin recalled. "I thought, 'Wow, this is like my family!'"

Auditioning for the sitcom was a long process. "I had four auditions, actually," Justin told the *Hollywood Reporter*. "I went to the casting director and Linwood the second time; the third time, I met with Linwood and Todd Holland [the show's co-executive producer/director]; and finally, it was the big network audition. There were about 20 people in one room, and everyone's staring at you, and it's really intimidating."

Even so, Justin nailed it and was hired to play the role of Reese, Malcolm's slightly older brother. Also cast were Frankie Muniz as the genius Malcolm, Erik Per Sullivan as baby of the family Dewey, and Christopher Masterson as Francis, the eldest brother. Bryan Cranston and Jane Kaczmarek were chosen to be their parents.

Reese was the role that would finally make Justin a household name.

Justin nailed the audition and was hired to play the role of Reese, Malcolm's slightly older brother.

A Home Away From Home

*M*alcolm in the Middle was an immediate hit. Justin thinks much of the show's success is due to the fact that all the actors genuinely like each other.

"We are very close," he said. "On a TV show, you can't fake chemistry. Everyone gets along so well. It's like a second family. All the kids talk to and relate to Bryan and Jane as if they were their own parents and all the kids get along as brothers. Since Erik has no siblings, Frankie and I took over the role of his big brothers."

That closeness extends to everyone on the crew. "About 90 percent of the crew this year is from the original season," Justin told the *Hollywood Reporter*. "So it's great; it's a big family."

Even though he plays Frankie's big brother on the show, Justin is actually two and a half months younger than Muniz. Because they're virtually the same age, they have a particularly close bond. They've literally grown up together on Malcolm. "We talk about everything," Justin said.

The closeness of the cast and crew was a new experience for Justin. So was the notoriety of being on such a popular show. He found himself on magazine covers and being called a "teen idol," a term which makes him uncomfortable. "I wouldn't consider myself one," he said in the teenhollywood.com chat. "What's the definition of a teen idol? I just consider myself an

Justin's castmates from Malcolm in the Middle *have become a second family to him. To celebrate the show's 100th episode, they threw a bowling party. From left to right: Gail Berman (former Entertainment President of FOX), Justin, Erik Per Sullivan, Bryan Cranston, Linwood Boomer (Executive Producer and Creator), Frankie Muniz, Jane Kaczmarek, Christopher Kennedy Masterson, Emy Coligado and Cloris Leachman.*

actor on a TV show, I don't know if anyone idolizes me."

Justin admits a lot more people recognize him now than when he was on *Unhappily Ever After*. "I enjoy it sometimes," he admitted. "I mean, it feels weird when you go into the public and you don't get recognized, because you wonder if anyone is still watching the show. So I guess it is a good thing when you do get recognized."

Even so, he doesn't consider that he is famous. And he hasn't had to worry about his privacy being invaded.

Justin and co-star Frankie Muniz have basically grown up together. Although they don't spend a lot of time away from the set together, Justin says he considers Frankie a brother. "We can literally talk about anything."

He joked that photographers hanging around his home in Malibu "are always knocking me over to get to Britney [Spears]."

However, the notoriety of being on a hit show did cause Justin problems at school. "I enjoyed going to regular school when I was younger because I enjoyed being around my friends," he said. "But once I got on *Malcolm in the Middle*, I couldn't go to regular school anymore. It was just too difficult. Malcolm is an incredibly popular show and it was difficult trying to be a normal kid when you kind of weren't. Everyone would always be asking questions about it in class. Once you hit high school, kids get a little more mean."

In real life Justin is known as a friendly, likable guy who gets along with everyone.

So although he was technically enrolled at Agoura High School, Justin spent a little more than a month going to class there. Instead, he was tutored on the set and completed his high school courses there.

It's more than a little ironic that Justin ended up becoming famous for playing a bully. In real life he's known as a friendly, likable guy who gets along with everyone. "I'm not loud like Reese and I don't go around beating people up," he laughed. He tried to explain in *Malibu Magazine* why Reese is the way he is. "He's a bully but he's misunderstood. He has a good heart but doesn't know how to express himself so he ends up just beating people up. That's how he expresses his emotions." But Justin added, "I love to play the character you love to hate!"

> *Justin loves playing Reese. "I have so much fun because he gets into so many crazy situations," he said.*

Unlike most sitcoms that are filmed entirely inside a sound stage on a studio lot, Malcolm frequently shoots episodes away from the set. This is called going on location. Justin's favorite episode was at a water park. "They shut down an entire park for us to film and then we all went on the slides after work," he said.

Although some actors say they get tired of playing the same character after so many years, Justin loves playing Reese. "I have so much fun because he gets into so many crazy situations," he said. "Bryan and I get to do the most fun stuff on the show. We're not the smartest characters so we get ourselves into crazy situations and get to do really fun things. I hope the show goes on for many more years."

When it does finally end, Justin will be ready to start the next phase of his career.

Branching Out

As soon as Justin turned eighteen, he moved into his own place. "I actually moved out when my brother did so it was kind of a shock to my mom," he laughed. He wanted to live closer to the studio where Malcolm is filmed so he wasn't spending so much time commuting. Then Justin bought a condominium in Malibu where he spends his weekends along with his dogs—a brown and white boxer named Divadog, a mutt named Fooz and his Chihuahua, Bean.

"I wanted to have a place to escape to when the city gets too crazy," he explained in *Malibu Magazine*. "It's fun to be there when you're working on the set but L.A. can be intense. I wanted a place where I could relax and chill and hang out with friends and walk on the beach. I really wanted to be on the ocean and take my dogs for a walk."

Justin also feels at home in Malibu because he and his dad used to fish there on weekends when he was growing up. "I always loved the area and loved the people because they are so nice," he said. "The second you get over the hill your stress level immediately drops because it's so peaceful and safe."

Although Justin is still the same animal-loving guy he was growing up, he's replaced his childhood dream of being a veterinarian with a new goal—to be a director and producer. He realizes that being on a series is a great way to learn all aspects of the entertainment business and is taking full advantage of the opportunity. "On set I'm really quiet," he said. "Instead of chatting it up between takes I'm always watching and listening. The wheels are spinning in my head all the time."

In 2004, Justin and his business partner, Jason Felts, formed a production company called J2 Entertainment. Their first venture was co-producing a musical comedy called *Romance and Cigarettes*. Released in 2005, the film stars James Gandolfini, Susan Sarandon, Kate Winslet and Mandy Moore. Justin and Jason also have a new reality

Justin and his business partner, Jason Felts, formed a production company called J2 Entertainment.

television series, *Filthy Rich: Cattle Drive*, in the works for the E! Entertainment Television cable channel. "I think eventually, after *Malcolm* is over and I have a little time, I'd like to go to college but right now I have no time," he said.

Despite his hectic schedule, he remains in close contact with his parents and brother. "We're a close-knit family," he said. "Even though I have my own place I still go out to dinner with them at least once a week."

Justin said his future plans include investing in more real estate—in addition to his homes in the Hollywood Hills and Malibu, he also bought a house in Dallas, Texas—and seeing the world. "When I have time off I love to travel," he said. "I go to the Cayman Islands all the time and to Cabo San Lucas, where my dad has a house. I went to Europe for the first time when I was 18 and saw London, Paris and Barcelona. Traveling is absolutely my favorite pastime."

Despite his hectic schedule, Justin remains in close contact with his parents and brother.

Beyond enjoying the financial freedom to travel and pursue his other goals, Justin is grateful at how much he's been able to experience thanks to being an actor. "There are a lot of things people on a TV show get to do that the general public never has the chance to," he told

Justin plans to have a long career — but not just as an actor. He and his business partner have formed a production company to develop television shows and feature films. His advice for anyone wanting to act is, "Just don't give up. You might go out on 100 interviews and you'll get maybe one. But don't give up."

the author. "Going to award shows like the Golden Globes and the Emmys are probably one of the biggest perks for me just because you know there are millions of people watching TV wishing they could be there. So I was grateful and appreciative I got to go there at such a young age. I appreciate those kinds of things now because who knows, in 20 years, I could be out of the business wishing I was back at the Emmys or Golden Globes."

Even though he didn't get to have a typical school experience and doesn't always get to hang out with friends because he's working, Justin says the sacrifices have been worth it. "Being an actor, I've been able to do more in my short life so far than a lot of people have done their entire lives," he said. "I don't think I've missed out on anything."

"Being an actor, I've been able to do more in my short life so far than a lot of people have done their entire lives."

1986	Born on February 25
1991	Lands first acting job in a Folgers Coffee commercial
1992	Gets first movie role in *3 Ninjas* but his part is cut out before the film's release
1994	Hired to co-star in first TV series, *The Good Life*
1995	Portrays Ross Malloy on the WB series *Unhappily Ever After*
1999	Cast as Reese on the FOX series *Malcolm in the Middle*
2000	Wins YoungStar Award for Best Ensemble in a TV Series with Frankie Muniz, Erik Per Sullivan and Christopher Masterson
2002	Is named youth ambassador for Ronald McDonald House Charities
2004	Forms his own production company called J2 Entertainment; co-produces first film, *Romance and Cigarettes*, which is released in 2005
2005	Executive produces his first reality television series entitled *Filthy Rich: Cattle Drive*

FOR FURTHER READING

Official Website
> http://www.officialjustinberfield.com

TV Tome – Justin Berfield
> http://www.tvtome.com/tvtome/servlet/PersonDetail/personid-1717

Live Event Chat – Justin Berfield
> http://teenmusic.com/transcripts.asp?event_id=1306Justin Berfield
> http://www.imdb.com/name/nm0073678/

Justin Berfield: A Real Crack Up during Celebrity Race
> http://blog.biggeststars.com/archives/2005/04/justin_berfield.html

Malcolm In the Middle — Official Website
> http://www.fox.com/malcolm/

ACTING AND PRODUCING

Acting	1994	*The Good Life* (TV series)
	1995	*Unhappily Ever After* (TV Series)
	1998	*Mom, Can I Keep Her?*
	1999	*The Kid with X-ray Eyes*
		Invisible Mom II (Video)
		Wanted
	2000	*Malcolm in the Middle* (TV series)
	2001	*Max Keeble's Big Move*
	2003	*Who's Your Daddy?*
Producing	2005	*Romance and Cigarettes*
		Filthy Rich: Cattle Drive (TV series)

INDEX